Practical
Recipes

Published by Blue Dome Press
535 Fifth Avenue, Ste. 601
New York, NY 10017-8019, USA

www.bluedomepress.com

Art Director Engin Çiftçi
Graphic Design Nihat İnce
Photographs Semih Ural

ISBN: 978-1-935295-48-8

Printed by
Imak Ofset, Istanbul - Turkey

Practical Recipes

in Turkish Cuisine

M. Ömür Akkor

New York

Contents

VEGETARIAN DISHES (MADE WITH OLIVE OIL)

MAIN DISHES

DESSERTS

Preface

Changing the World and Traditional Cuisines

French philosopher Jean Baudrillard discusses in his book, *The Transparency of Evil*, concepts such as aesthetics, politics, the economy, and art. He explains that these different concepts intermingle; they are no longer independent like in the past. For example, today's art is a "trans-art" that has political, economic, and aesthetic components. Similarly, I believe that this intermingling is true of food and culture.

Foods on our dining table are not authentic enough anymore. Recipes are now altered as a result of globalization, the economy, and cultural convergence. Fast food chains and globalization has had a dramatic impact on food culture. Because of globalization, people are curious about the cuisine of different cultures in different geographies. This curiosity has led to the opening of various international restaurants and the sharing of different ingredients. Thanks to this, authentic cuisines are protected to some degree and the recipes which may have been forgotten are recorded. The intellectual progress and establishment of social awareness on this issue is one of my biggest wishes.

Every passing day we encounter products with extended shelf-lives and nonperishable benefits. Some examples are sugars which can merge into the blood faster, foods that are supposed to make you full but actually make you more hungry, and fake products marketed as real foods such as sweeteners, thickeners etc. In fact, the science of molecular gastronomy has emerged as a reflection of this commercial development. Now chefs are cooking in laboratories instead of in their kitchens and are developing foods which are manipulated structurally. People have already learned that the consumption of these structurally degenerated foods can cause many diseases. In response, the demand for organic products and non-processed foods has increased, just not enough.

Another food related issue revolves around garnishing. The major difference between Western and Eastern cuisine is the emphasis placed upon the appearance of food. In our culture, food primarily has an ethical meaning. As a matter of fact, we have numerous idioms such as: "dad's furnace," "sharing the bread," "bringing salt to the table," "sitting around the same dining table," and "feeding the hungry." Food in Islamic culture is a blessing; moreover, bread is sacred. Even stale bread would not be thrown into the trash but used in cooking. In our culture, meaning comes first and later comes the taste. Frivolity is not allowed around the dinner table as the blessing of food is respected and the meal is eaten with gratitude. For this reason, the way the food is displayed is not of huge significance to our culture. The spectacular feasts prepared by François Vatel, a very famous example from the traditional Western cuisine, seem to prove the difference between our cuisines. In the Western culture, food decoration is substantial in meal preparation. The dining table is a place to chat, to watch shows, and to have fun.

As I have written in the preface of my book, *Bursa Cuisine*, food travels from one location to another the same way people do. During these journeys, wherever it reaches it gets enriched via the influence of life conditions in those specific geographies. Turkish cuisine was enriched by interacting with other cultures in the Western and Islamic regions from the time of their arrival in Anatolia till today. I think the interaction of cuisines is more than just imitation. While the effects of the interaction are positive, the effects of imitation are negative. As an executive chef, I am watching, with sorrow and anxiety, the degradation of our original recipes and cuisine by mixing the title of meals, the cooking styles, and the ingredients from very different cuisines with traditional ones. However, I also would like to mention that by all means I am not against the creativity, the quest for taste, and the use of different ingredients. Needless to say, experimental studies and the different presentation of plates should be practiced in the kitchen. Nevertheless, everybody is responsible for protecting their own cuisine and culture from assimilation.

Turkish Culinary Culture

Throughout the centuries, Turks were traditionally horsemen and nomads. One of the fundamental effects of this lifestyle can be found in Turkish food culture. The Turks traveled with their horses and hair tents, adapting to the various climates, circumstances, and conditions. Sometimes they brought their culture to the new location and other times they collated their culture with what they took. This fast-paced life and rapid change developed and diversified their cultural structure. The Turks had taken a distinct stance and implemented the formation of a very comprehensive culture which had an impact on the whole world.

In the beginning, Turkish food culture distinguished itself as being easy to prepare and storable. Later on, it was altered according to the geographical conditions of the region they traveled to. However, the Turks absolutely never forgot where they came from and the culture they had brought. Wherever they stopped, they encountered new ingredients. These new ingredients were incorporated into their kitchen and led to fantastic recipes. Sometimes they altered a recipe by replacing an ingredient which they could not find with a new one; as a result, they created their own recipes wherever they were located.

When they departed from Middle Asia and reached the Balkans, they were no longer the Turks that they were at the beginning of their journey. Turkish people endured massive difficulties and challenges during this journey, which lasted many miles and many years. In the end, the remainder of these obstacles was the Turkish culture with its great heritage. Perhaps it is not possible to know exactly what they used to eat when they first stepped out of Middle Asia on their horses; however, what Turkish people eat today is quite obvious.

Speaking of Turkish Cuisine...

Turkish cuisine is not only found within the borders of Turkey. When we say Turkish cuisine, we should think not only of the cuisine of Turkish people who live in Turkey, but also the cuisine of all people with a Turkish identity. We may extend the same example for Anatolia. At the present time, even though we describe it as the cuisine of people who live in Anatolia, Anatolian cuisine consists of the cuisine of various civilizations, such as the Hittites, Seljuks, and Romans. Anatolia's geography, vegetation, and other conditions have remained the same for thousands of years. That is why it is possible to come across the same dessert from the time of the Hittites in Çorum or Bursa.

Food is a large component of any culture, and it is up to us to protect it under any circumstance. At the same time, we must continue to expand and differentiate ourselves. Take the Turks and the Anatolians for example. Some have more abundant amounts of wheat and they use that to make their bread, whereas others have more abundant amounts of corn. Either way, they are all eating bread.

My wish is that cuisines of the world accept change while embracing authenticity. My purpose in this book is to share my Turkish culinary culture and recipes which are healthy, practical, and can be prepared in a very short time in your kitchen.

May the salt of your dinner table and the peace of your home not be lacking.

Measurement Table

1 cup water or milk = 250 ml

1 cup molasses = 250 g

1 cup granulated sugar, wheat, bean, lentil or rice = 200 g

1 cup flour = 140 g

1 tablespoon granulated sugar = 15 g

1 tablespoon butter = 15 g

1 tablespoon paprika paste =15 g

1 tablespoon flour = 15 g

1 tablespoon olive oil = 15 g

1 teaspoon salt =6 g

1 teaspoon black or red pepper = 3 g

Red Lentil and Mint Soup

(Ezogelin Çorbası)

1 tablespoon flour

2 tablespoons butter

1 tablespoon tomato paste

1 tablespoon sweet pepper paste

2 tablespoons dried mint

1 tablespoon red pepper flakes

1 tablespoon salt

½ pound boiled red lentils

6 cups water

Brown the flour with the butter in a large saucepan. After 2 minutes, add the pastes and spices. Sauté together for 1 minute. Add the red lentil and water. Leave it to boil. When the soup starts to boil, turn the heat down to simmer for 10 minutes and serve. If you wish, you can add 1 tablespoon bulgur or rice while the red lentil is boiling.

Serves 4 to 6.

Yogurt and Mint Soup
(Yayla Çorbası)

2 oz. rice

1 teaspoon salt

4 cups water

1 egg

2 pound yogurt

1 tablespoon flour

6 tablespoons olive oil

2 tablespoons dried mint

½ teaspoon black pepper

Rinse and drain the rice, put it in a large saucepan, and bring it to a boil in four cups of salted water for 25 minutes. Meanwhile, in a medium saucepan, scramble the egg and thoroughly combine with the yogurt and flour. Make the yogurt mix warm by gradually adding several scoops of the water from the boiled rice. Continue to heat up the yogurt mix by stirring it continually on low heat. When steam begins to rise from the yogurt mix, turn off the heat and pour over the boiling rice. Stir the soup a few more times and then turn the heat off. Afterwards, warm the olive oil in a skillet without burning it and add the dried mint and black pepper. Pour it over the soup and serve hot.

Serves 4 to 6.

Cold Wheat Soup

(Soğuk Buğday Çorbası)

1 pound strained yogurt

2 cups water

1 bunch dill

4 tablespoons sweet basil

1 teaspoon salt

1 tablespoon dried mint

1 pound wheat, boiled

Thoroughly mix the yogurt and water in a large bowl. Chop the dill and basil finely and add them into the yogurt. Add the salt, dried mint, and wheat into the yogurt mix and stir everything. Serve cold. If you wish, you can add ice into the soup. You can serve this soup with a selection of greens as well as boiled spinach.

Serves 4 to 6.

Creamy Chicken Broth Soup

(Terbiyeli Tavuk Suyu Çorbası)

2 cups chicken broth

2 cups water

5 tablespoons orzo

1 teaspoon salt

½ teaspoon black pepper

2 lemons, juice extracted

1 egg

Combine chicken broth and water and bring to a boil in a medium saucepan. When the chicken broth boils, add the orzo into it. Add the salt and black pepper. Cook for 10 minutes on low heat. Meanwhile, beat the lemon juice and egg nicely in a mixing bowl and gradually stir this mixture into the boiling soup. Leave it to boil for a few more minutes and turn the heat off. Serve hot.

You can cook this soup with chicken, which is boiled and pulled apart into little pieces. You may also serve it with sprinkled parsley.

Serves 4 to 6.

Spicy Red Pepper Dip
(Muhammara)

1 pound fresh red peppers

2 garlic cloves

1 bowl stale bread or rusk

1 teaspoon cumin

1 teaspoon salt

¼ bowl walnut, crushed and chopped

5 tablespoons olive oil

3 tablespoons pomegranate molasses

Cut open the red peppers, remove the seeds, and stems and chop them coarsely. In a food processor blend together the peppers, garlic, stale bread, cumin, and salt until the mixture is left fairly coarse. Then transfer the *muhammara* to a large mixing bowl and add the crushed walnuts, olive oil, and pomegranate molasses. You can either serve it on a serving dish or on bread. You may sprinkle crushed walnuts on top if you wish.

Serves 6 to 8.

Splendid Hummus
(Humus-u Ala)

2 bowls chickpeas, boiled

3 garlic cloves

¼ cup *tahini*

2 tablespoons olive oil

1 teaspoon cumin

¼ cup water

1 teaspoon salt

For the salad:

½ onion

2 medium tomatoes

½ bunch arugula

½ bunch dill

5 pickles

4 tablespoons beet, pickled

5 tablespoons pomegranate molasses

5 tablespoons olive oil

Put the boiled chickpeas, garlic, *tahini*, olive oil, cumin, water, and salt in a food processor. Mix all the ingredients in the food processor until they are smooth. Meanwhile, begin preparing the salad by chopping onion, tomatoes, arugula, and dill fairly large. Place the hummus on a serving plate. Add the salad that you prepared over the hummus. Set the pickles on the very top. Finally, add the pomegranate molasses and olive oil and serve.

You can make sandwiches with the left over hummus or store it in the storage box in the refrigerator for a couple of days to make salad again.

Serves 6 to 8.

Aegean Dipping Sauce
(Ege Ezmesi)

1 pound white cheese (*feta*)

2 tablespoons ground pistachios

1 garlic clove, pounded

1 bunch parsley, minced

1 bunch dill, minced

¼ pound strained yogurt

2 tablespoons olive oil

If the cheese is salty, thoroughly rinse and drain it. Put the cheese in a large mixing bowl and squash completely with the help of a fork. Add the pistachios, garlic, greens, and yogurt over the cheese. Mix everything nicely and add olive oil. Place on a serving plate and drizzle olive oil on top.

If you wish, you can also serve with croutons. You can also prepare this recipe with the addition of tomatoes and walnuts.

Serves 6 to 8.

Shakshouka

(Şakşuka)

4 medium eggplants
1 medium potato
1 medium zucchini
2 red peppers
4 green peppers
½ cup olive oil
1 teaspoon salt
3 medium tomatoes, puréed
3 garlic cloves, minced
½ teaspoon black pepper
1 teaspoon granulated sugar
1 bunch parsley, minced

Peel the eggplants and potato. Chop zucchini, red and green peppers in equal-sized cubes (⅓ inch x ⅓ inch). Spread the vegetables on to wax paper. Add almost all of the olive oil and sprinkle some salt on the vegetables. Bake the prepared vegetables at 190°C (375°F) in a preheated oven for 30 minutes. Open the oven door two times while the vegetables are cooking and stir them. Meanwhile, pour the rest of the olive oil in a skillet and turn the heat on medium. First add the garlic cloves and the tomato purée to the skillet. Then add the salt, black pepper, and sugar and sauté for 10 minutes on low heat. Finally add the vegetables just out of the oven into the tomato sauce and cook for 2 more minutes all together, and then place on the serving plate. Sprinkle minced parsley to garnish and serve.

Although it is usually consumed hot, in Turkish cuisine it can also be served after it has cooled.

Serves 6.

Fine Bulgur Salad
(Kısır)

1 medium onion

1 teaspoon flaked red pepper

1 teaspoon dried mint

2 tablespoons tomato paste

2 tablespoons pepper paste

1 teaspoon salt

2 ½ cups bulgur, fine-grain

1 cup warm water

2 medium tomatoes

¼ pound pickles

1 bunch parsley, finely minced

⅓ cup olive oil

¼ cup pomegranate molasses

Dice the onion finely. Combine the onion, red pepper, mint, tomato and pepper paste, and salt to the bulgur and pour hot water over top. Cover the bulgur and leave it to rest for 10 minutes. Meanwhile, slice the tomatoes into small cubes and pickles into circles. After the bulgur rests for 10 minutes, add the parsley, tomato, olive oil, and pomegranate molasses and knead for 5 minutes. Lastly, add the pickles and serve.

Turkish bulgur salad is indispensable at teatimes. It can be served plain or with boiled cabbage, lettuce, or grape leaves.

Serves 6 to 8.

Shepherd's Salad

(Çoban Salata)

3 medium tomatoes

2 medium cucumbers

1 medium onion

2 green peppers

½ bunch parsley, minced

1 lemon, juice extracted

½ teaspoon salt

4 tablespoons olive oil

Dice the tomatoes, cucumbers, onion, and peppers into cubes and put in a medium mixing bowl. Add the parsley into the salad. Combine the lemon juice, salt, and olive oil and add to the salad. Toss the salad and serve. If you wish, you can also add 1 tablespoon vinegar to this salad.

Serves 4.

Tomato Salad with Walnuts and Cumin

(Gavurdağı Salatası)

5 medium tomatoes

2 medium cucumbers

1 medium onion

2 red peppers

2 green peppers

½ bunch parsley, minced

¼ bunch fresh mint, minced

1 teaspoon dried mint

1 teaspoon sumac

1 teaspoon salt

¼ pound walnuts, crushed and chopped

5 tablespoons pomegranate molasses

½ bowl pomegranate, granulated

7 tablespoons olive oil

Chop tomatoes, cucumbers, onion, red and green peppers into cubes and put in a large mixing bowl. Add the parsley, fresh and dried mint, sumac and salt into the salad. Add walnuts, pomegranate molasses, pomegranate grains, and olive oil then serve.

(Gavurdağı is one of the summits of the Taurus Mountains in the Mediterranean region of Turkey. This salad is a favorite at the roadside restaurants in the region. Although it does have various recipes and the ingredients may change depending on the season, pomegranate molasses, crushed walnuts, and dried mint are necessary ingredients in this salad.)

Serves 4 to 6.

Spicy Dipping Sauce

(Acılı Ezme)

4 medium tomatoes

2 medium cucumbers

1 medium onion

1 red pepper

3 long green peppers

1 bunch parsley, minced

2 tablespoons pepper paste

2 tablespoons tomato paste

1 teaspoon black pepper

1 teaspoon salt

8 tablespoons pomegranate molasses

8 tablespoons olive oil

Peel the tomatoes, cucumbers, and onion. Cut off the top of the peppers and deseed them. Mince all the ingredients, and combine them in a large mixing bowl. Add the parsley, tomato and pepper pastes, black pepper, salt, pomegranate molasses, and olive oil over the mix. Stir to combine, place the salad on a large serving plate and drizzle with some additional olive oil.

If you leave the spicy dipping sauce in the refrigerator for a few hours, it will become even more delicious. Note that you can chop all the vegetables in a food processor for faster preparation.

Serves 6.

Yogurt with Cucumber
(Cacık)

1 pound crispy cucumbers

1 pound strained yogurt

5 tablespoons olive oil

1 garlic clove, pounded

1 teaspoon salt

1 tablespoon dried mint

¼ cup water

Dice or shred the cucumbers (if you wish, without peeling them). Whip the yogurt and olive oil together in a large mixing bowl for 3 minutes. Add the garlic clove, salt, dried mint, and water. Finally, mix the yogurt and the cucumbers together and pour into serving bowls. Drizzle olive oil and dried mint over it. You should serve it with ice, especially in the summer.

Serves 4 to 6.

Potato Salad

(Patates Salatası)

5 medium potatoes, boiled

3 eggs, boiled

2 medium tomatoes

1 bunch parsley, finely minced

1 bunch green onion, finely minced

2 lemons, juice extracted

¼ cup olive oil

1 teaspoon red pepper flakes

1 teaspoon salt

Peel the potatoes and eggs. Dice the potatoes, eggs and tomatoes into cubes and put into a large bowl. Add the parsley, green onion, lemon juice, olive oil, red pepper flakes, and salt to the mixture. Stir the mixture nicely and serve.

Serves 4 to 6.

Roasted Pepper Rolls with Cheese
(Peynirli Közlenmiş Biber Dolması)

¼ pound white cheese (*feta*)

2 tablespoons labneh cheese

2 tablespoons parsley, minced

2 tablespoons dill, minced

5 red peppers, roasted

10 to 12 chives or parsley stems

1 teaspoon extra-virgin olive oil

Mash the white cheese with the help of a fork in a medium mixing bowl. Prepare a stuffing by combining the white cheese with labneh, dill, and parsley. Cut the red peppers in half vertically. As if you are making stuffed grape leaves, put half of the pepper on the cutting board flat and after placing some of the stuffing roll them over. Repeat the same thing until you finish stuffing all the peppers. Leave the chives or parsley stems in the hot water for 3 minutes to soften. Wrap the rolls with greens and tie, and transfer to the serving plate. Lastly, drizzle with olive oil and serve.

Serves 4.

Turkish Green Beans
(Taze Fasulye)

1 pound green beans

3 medium tomatoes

1 medium onion

1 teaspoon salt

1 teaspoon granulated sugar

¼ cup hot water

¼ cup olive oil

Coarsely chop green beans and put into the pot. Peel the tomatoes, remove their seeds, and cut them into large pieces. Chop the onion finely and add to the tomatoes, then combine with the green beans. Add salt, sugar, water, and olive oil. Place the pot on the stove, and when it starts to boil, lower the heat and cook for 40 minutes. Then, turn off the heat and set aside. Serve cool (preferably after keeping it in the refrigerator for one day).

Serves 4.

Kidney Beans in Olive Oil
(Zeytinyağlı Barbunya)

1 medium potato

2 medium carrots

1 medium onion

¼ cup olive oil

4 garlic cloves, finely minced

2 tablespoon celery stalk, chopped

1 teaspoon granulated sugar

1 teaspoon salt

1 tablespoon tomato paste

1 tomato, puréed

1 pound kidney beans, boiled

¼ cup hot water

Dice potato and the carrots in small cubes. Chop the onion and sauté with olive oil in a medium saucepan. After a few minutes, add the potato, carrots, garlic, celery stalk, sugar, salt, and tomato paste. Fry everything together for 5 minutes, and after adding the tomato purée, boiled kidney beans, and water, let cook for 20 minutes. It can be served warm or cold. You may garnish with parsley and lemon if you wish.

Serves 4.

Boiled Artichokes
(Enginar)

6 artichokes, peeled

½ pound boiled carrot, potatoes, and green peas

1 teaspoon flour

1 lemon, juice extracted

¼ cup olive oil

¼ cup hot water

1 teaspoon salt

4 teaspoons dill, minced

Line the artichokes side by side in a large pot. Sprinkle the carrot, potatoes and green peas equally over the artichokes. Mix the flour, lemon juice, and olive oil separately in a small bowl, and then pour over the dish. Add hot water and place pot on the stove. Cook for 30 minutes. Serve warm or cold. Sprinkle with dill before serving.

Serves 6.

Sour Okra with Chickpeas
(Ekşili Zeytinyağlı Bamya)

1 medium onion

3 medium tomatoes

½ cup hot water

1 teaspoon powdered essence of lemon

1 pound okra, stem end trimmed

5 garlic cloves, finely minced

¼ pound chickpeas, boiled

¼ cup olive oil

1 teaspoon salt

Chop the onion into small cubes. Peel the tomatoes and cut into cubes. Put the hot water in a medium bowl, add the powdered essence of lemon, and let it melt. Put the olive oil in a medium saucepan and sauté the onion. After frying 2 minutes, add the okra, garlic cloves, chickpeas, and tomatoes. Add the powdered essence of lemon melted in the hot water, and salt. Lower the heat and close the lid. Cook for approximately 30 minutes without stirring. Set aside for a few minutes before serving.

Serves 4.

Arugula with Beets
(Pancarlı Zeytinyağlı Roka)

2 bunches arugula

½ bunch dill

2 cups water

¼ pound beets, pickled or boiled

2 lemons, juice extracted

1 teaspoon salt

3 garlic cloves, minced

⅓ cup olive oil

Coarsely chop the arugula and dill. Put the water in a large saucepan and bring to a boil. Add the arugula and dill, cook for 3 minutes, and then strain. Rinse well with cold water and strain again. Place the arugula and dill on a serving plate. Finely mince the pickled (or boiled) beets and add them over the arugula. Combine the lemon juice, salt, garlic cloves, and olive oil in a medium bowl to make a dressing and stir. Drizzle with the dressing and serve.

In the Aegean region of Turkey, this recipe is the common way to prepare vegetarian dishes made with olive oil. Depending on the type of boiled herbs, they might be served with the dressing mentioned above or with yogurt.

Serves 4.

Zucchini Fritters
(Mücver)

4 medium zucchinis

½ bunch parsley, minced

½ bunch green onions, minced

1 bunch dill, minced

4 eggs

4 tablespoons flour

1 teaspoon salt

½ teaspoon black pepper

2 tablespoons olive oil

Sesame seeds

Grate the zucchinis in a deep mixing bowl. Add the minced parsley, green onions, and dill over the zucchinis. Break the eggs over the mixture. After adding the flour, salt, and black pepper, stir to combine. Oil a mini muffin tray with the olive oil and fill the cups halfway with the prepared mixture. Sprinkle with sesame seeds. Bake at 180ºC (350°F) in a preheated oven for 20 minutes, and serve with yogurt if you wish.

Serves 4.

Chickpeas with Sausage
(Sucuklu Nohut)

1 medium onion

3 tablespoons butter

2 medium tomatoes

2 green peppers

2 tablespoons tomato paste

1 pound chickpeas, boiled

½ teaspoon black pepper

½ teaspoon red pepper flakes

1 teaspoon salt

2 cups water

20 slices sausage

Dice the onion, tomatoes, and peppers. Fry the onion by using one tablespoon of butter in a medium saucepan. Add the green peppers, tomatoes, and tomato paste into the frying onion. After frying the vegetables for about 5 minutes, add the chickpeas, spices, and water; bring to a boil. Cook for 15 minutes at medium heat. Meanwhile, fry the sausages with the remaining butter and add to the vegetable mixture. Cook for 5 more minutes at low heat.
Serve with dried hot peppers if desired.

Serves 4 to 6.

Noodles with Walnuts
(Cevizli Erişte)

2 cups water

1 pound noodles

2 tablespoons butter

¼ pound walnuts, crushed

¼ pound *tulum* (skin bag) cheese

2 tablespoons parsley, minced

2 tablespoons dill, minced

1 tablespoon salt

Put the water in a medium saucepan and bring to a boil. Add the noodles, cook for 8 minutes, and strain them. Fry the butter in a medium pan for a few minutes, add the walnuts, and turn the heat off. Put the strained noodles into a bowl. Add the *tulum* cheese, the butter with walnuts, parsley, dill, and salt and serve.

Serves 4.

Pilaf
(Pilav)

2 cups rice

3 cups water

3 tablespoons butter

1 teaspoon salt

½ teaspoon black pepper

Soak rice in hot water for 15 minutes. Afterwards, rinse the rice with plenty of water. Melt butter in a pot and add the rice. Fry for 3 minutes then add three cups of water and salt. When the water starts to boil, lower the heat and cook for about 10 minutes until the rice absorbs all the water. Let it rest for 10 minutes and serve with black pepper.

Rice pilaf is one of the essential recipes in Turkish cuisine and it can be prepared plain as explained above or with chicken, chickpeas, or orzo.

Serves 4 to 6.

Pilaf with Tomatoes
(Domatesli Pilav)

3 medium tomatoes

2 garlic cloves, minced

4 tablespoons olive oil

1 ½ cups rice

1 teaspoon salt

½ teaspoon black pepper

1 teaspoon granulated sugar

½ bunch arugula, minced

½ bunch parsley, minced

½ bunch dill, minced

½ bunch green onions, thinly sliced

2 tablespoons butter

Peel and dice tomatoes into cubes. Sauté the garlic with olive oil and add the tomatoes in a large saucepan. Then add the rice, salt, black pepper and sugar. After it starts to boil, lower the heat and cook for 15 minutes by continuously stirring until the water boils down. When the rice cooks, turn the heat off and add all the arugula, parsley, dill, green onions, and the butter. Give one final stir and serve.

Serves 4 to 6.

Bulgur Pilaf with Vegetables
(Sebzeli Bulgur Pilavı)

2 medium eggplants

3 medium tomatoes

2 green peppers

2 red peppers

3 tablespoons butter

2 tablespoons olive oil

1 garlic clove

2 tablespoons sweet pepper paste

2 tablespoons dried mint

½ teaspoon black pepper

1 teaspoon salt

1 ½ cups bulgur, medium-grain

1 cup chickpeas, boiled

3 cups water

Peel the eggplants and dice into 1-inch cubes. Dice the tomatoes and peppers into smaller cubes. Melt the butter with olive oil in a medium saucepan. When the oil heats up, add the eggplants; after 7 minutes, add the peppers, and then sauté for 5 minutes. Slice the head of garlic in half and combine with the pepper paste, tomatoes, mint, black pepper and salt; sauté for 5 more minutes. Lastly, add the bulgur, chickpeas, and water, then bring it to a boil. When the water boils, lower the heat and cook for about 20 minutes until the liquid evaporates. Turn off the heat and let it rest for 10 minutes before serving.

Serves 4 to 6.

Pan-Fried Calf's Liver
(Ciğer Tava)

1 cup oil for frying

½ pound flour

1 teaspoon salt

1 pound calf's liver, in small chunks

For the salad:

2 medium onions

2 medium tomatoes

½ bunch parsley

1 lemon, juice extracted

4 tablespoons olive oil

½ teaspoon sumac

1 teaspoon salt

Warm the oil in a large and deep pan. Mix the flour and salt in a bowl. Roll the livers in the flour and fry them for about 4 minutes. Transfer the fried livers from the pan onto paper towel to remove excess oil. Slice the onions into crescent shapes and dice the tomatoes into cubes. Mince the parsley and combine all of the salad ingredients with the lemon juice, olive oil, sumac, and salt in a mixing bowl, and then transfer to a serving plate. Place the fried liver alongside the salad and serve.

Serves 4.

Roasted Eggplant Purée with Yogurt and Meat

(Ali Nazik)

1 pound eggplant, roasted

2 garlic cloves, pounded

1 teaspoon salt

1 pound strained yogurt

2 tablespoons butter

½ pound ground lamb

1 red pepper, finely chopped

2 green peppers, finely chopped

1 tablespoon sweet red pepper paste

½ teaspoon red pepper flakes

½ teaspoon black pepper

2 tablespoons parsley, minced

Finely chop the roasted eggplant and put it in a deep mixing bowl. Add the garlic, salt, and yogurt, mix them thoroughly, and set aside. In a large pan, sauté the ground lamb and peppers in butter for 10 minutes then add the paste, red and black pepper. Sauté for 3 more minutes and turn the heat off. Lay the eggplant and yogurt mix on a large serving plate and put the ground lamb mix over it. Sprinkle minced parsley over the dish.

This recipe can be prepared with chicken chunks, lamb chunks, ground beef or veal tenderloin steak.

Serves 4 to 6.

Kebabs with Pita
(Pideli Kebap)

4 small pitas or stale bread

1 medium tomato or ½ bowl cherry tomatoes

3 tablespoons butter

1 pound fillet steaks, thinly sliced

2 tablespoons olive oil

1 teaspoon tomato paste

1 teaspoon salt

½ teaspoon black pepper

1 pound strained yogurt, whisked

Cut the pitas and the tomatoes into cubes and fry in one tablespoon of butter, in a large pan. In another pan, sauté the steaks in the remaining butter and olive oil. Add tomato paste, salt, black pepper, and steaks. Put the pitas on a serving plate, top with steaks, and drizzle the whisked yogurt. You may garnish with fried peppers and tomatoes if you wish.

Serves 4.

Pastry with Spinach
(Ispanaklı Börek)

1 pound spinach

3 sheets of phyllo dough

½ pound quark cheese

½ pound white cheese (*feta*), grated

3 eggs

1 cup olive oil

1 cup soda water

1 cup milk

Chop the spinach into 1 inch pieces and place in a large and deep mixing bowl. Cut a sheet of phyllo dough in half; set aside one half. Crumble the other half with your hands and add to the spinach. Add the quark and *feta* cheese to this bowl as well.

In another bowl, whisk the eggs, milk, and oil. Then add the soda water. Add this mixture to the spinach mixture and combine. Slightly oil a deep baking pan about thirty centimeters in size and begin to layer the phyllo dough sheets by putting spinach stuffing in the middle. Place the layer at the bottom in such a way that it could cover the sides of the pastry. Bake at 180°C (350°F) in a preheated oven for 30 minutes until golden brown. Serve warm.

Serves 6 to 8.

Pizza with Spicy Meat Filling
(Kolay Lahmacun)

2 medium onions, chopped
1 pound ground beef
2 tablespoons butter
2 medium tomatoes, puréed
1 tablespoon tomato paste
1 green pepper, minced
1 red pepper, minced
1 bunch parsley, minced
1 teaspoon cumin
½ teaspoon black pepper
½ teaspoon red pepper flakes
1 teaspoon salt
4 lavash or tortillas

For serving

1 bunch parsley, trimmed
1 lemon, sliced

Sauté the ground beef in butter in a large pan for 3 minutes. Stir in the tomato purée, tomato paste, and minced peppers. Sauté ingredients for 3 minutes then turn the heat off.

Add the parsley, cumin, black and red pepper, and leave it to rest for 5 minutes. Spread this mixture on the tortillas and bake at 200°C (400°F) in a preheated oven for 5 minutes until tortillas become crisp. Serve with parsley and lemon.

Serves 4.

Oven Baked Kebabs
(Tava Kebabı)

1 medium onion

2 medium tomatoes

4 green peppers

2 red peppers

1 pound fillet steak chunks

2 tomatoes, grated

1 tablespoon tomato paste

1 teaspoon thyme

½ teaspoon black pepper

1 teaspoon salt

4 tablespoons olive oil

3 tablespoons butter

Chop the onion, tomatoes, and peppers into cubes and sauté. Blend this with the fillet steak chunks, grated tomatoes, tomato paste, thyme, black pepper, salt, oil, and butter in a deep bowl. Spread the mixture on a flat, broad, and shallow baking pot. Bake at 200°C (400°F) in a preheated oven for 20 minutes. While the kabobs are cooking open the oven door once and stir up the mixture. When it's ready, place the baking pot directly on the dinner table to serve.

Serves 4 to 6.

White Beans with Pastrami
(Pastırmalı Kuru Fasulye)

1 medium onion

2 green peppers

1 red pepper

4 tablespoons butter

2 tablespoon tomato paste

1 tablespoon sweet pepper paste

2 medium tomatoes, grated

1 pound white beans, boiled

1 ½ cups water

½ teaspoon black pepper

1 teaspoon salt

10 slices pastrami

Dice the onion into cubes. Mince the peppers. Sauté the onion with one tablespoon of butter in a medium saucepan (or in a clay pot, if possible). After 5 minutes, stir in the peppers, tomato paste and pepper paste. Then add the grated tomatoes and boiled white beans. Add water, black pepper, and salt, then leave it to cook for 20 minutes. Melt 2 tablespoons of butter in a skillet. Stir in the pastrami and sauté for one minute. Transfer to the boiling white beans. After boiling a few more minutes, turn the heat off and serve.

Serves 4 to 6.

Meatballs with Vegetables
(Sebzeli Köfte)

4 slices stale bread

1 medium onion, chopped

4 tablespoons parsley, minced

1 pound ground beef, suitable to make meatballs

1 egg

2 tablespoons tomato paste

1 teaspoon cumin

½ teaspoon black pepper

1 teaspoon salt

2 tablespoons butter

1 pound boiled carrots, potatoes and green peas, ready to use

1 cup water

Crumble the stale bread. Knead the onion, parsley, ground beef, egg, crumbled bread, and one tablespoon of tomato paste, cumin, black pepper, and salt in a deep bowl. Shape into walnut sized meatballs. Fry the meatballs with butter in a skillet. Add the remaining tomato paste over the meatballs. After a few minutes, add the boiled carrot, potatoes, green peas, and water. Cook at medium heat for 10 minutes and serve.

Serves 4 to 6.

Chicken Stew
(Tavuk Haşlama)

1 medium onion

4 medium potatoes

2 medium carrots

1 celery stalk

4 chicken legs

½ teaspoon black pepper

1 teaspoon salt

3 cups water

Chop the onion, potatoes, and carrots into a few pieces. Thinly slice celery stalk. Place the chicken legs, vegetables, black pepper, salt, and water in a medium pot. Cook for 30 minutes with the lid closed and serve. Chicken stew is considered a culinary curative in Turkish cuisine.

Serves 4.

Shepherd's Fried Meat
(Çoban Kavurma)

1 medium onion

2 medium tomatoes

2 green peppers

1 red pepper

2 tablespoons butter

1 pound fillet steak chunks

3 tablespoons olive oil

1 teaspoon salt

½ teaspoon black pepper

Lavash (soft, thin flat bread)

Chop the onion, tomatoes, green and red peppers into small cubes. In a hot skillet, melt the butter. Add the onion, steak, salt, and black pepper; sauté for 5 minutes. Add the tomatoes, green and red peppers and cook for 10 more minutes; serve with lavash.

Serves 4 to 6.

Rice Pudding
(Sütlaç)

4 cups milk

⅓ pound granulated sugar

4 tablespoons butter

¼ pound cream

¼ cup corn starch

¼ cup milk

¼ pound boiled white rice

6 clay pots or souffle cups

Mix the 4 cups milk, sugar, butter, and cream in a pot and bring it to a boil. In a bowl, blend the corn starch and ¼ cup milk and add this mixture to the boiling one. Boil ingredients for 2 more minutes. Combine ingredients with the boiled rice, distribute equally into six oven-safe pots or cups. Place them onto a deep baking pan filled with water to half its depth. Bake at a 240°C (464°F) in a preheated oven for 10 minutes until golden brown. Take the bowls out of the oven after 10 minutes and let cool before serving.

Serves 6.

Paradise Mud

(Cennet Çamuru)

2 pound granulated sugar

2 pound water

1 slice lemon

1 pound *kadayıf* (string-shaped dough)

½ pound butter

½ pound pistachios, ground

10 tablespoons cream or ice-cream

1 teaspoon cinnamon

Mix the sugar and water into a medium pot and bring it to a boil. When the sherbet boils, throw in one slice of lemon and turn the heat off. Leave the sherbet to cool down. Shred the *kadayıf*, cut them into 1 inch pieces, and put in a large pan. Melt the butter, add it to the *kadayıf*, and fry it for 20 minutes. Turn the heat off and stir in the pistachios. Pour the sherbet over the *kadayıf*. After 10 minutes, serve it with cream or ice cream. Sprinkle with cinnamon. Heaven's mud can sit for a couple of days; however, at each serving you should warm it up with some sherbet.

Serves 10.

Curd Cheese Dessert with Jam

(Reçelli Lor Tatlısı)

½ cup milk

½ pound curd cheese, unsalted

1 jar blackberry jam (or any other jam)

Blend the milk with cheese in a food processor until smooth. Divide this mixture at the bottom of the serving bowls and serve them with the blackberry jam on top. This dessert can be prepared not only with the blackberry jam, but also with other jams or fresh fruits.

Serves 6 to 8.

Butternut Squash Dessert
(Kabak Tatlısı)

1 pound butternut squash, peeled

3 cups granulated sugar

¼ cup water

For serving:

¼ pound cream

¼ pound walnuts, crushed and chopped

¼ pound *tahini*

Slice the squash and place in a large pot side by side. Add sugar and water. Cook at low heat for 30 minutes.

After it cools down, you may serve it with cream, chopped walnuts or *tahini*. If you have time, sprinkle sugar over the squash and leave it overnight. Then the following morning, cook it in its own liquid.

Serves 8.